			⏳ ya = years ago
			mya = million years ago

Page	Mammal	Spot	Extinction period ⏳	Closest relative(s)
14	**Glyptodon** ("carved tooth")	Christ the Redeemer, Rio de Janeiro, Brazil	Late Pleistocene (11,000 ya)	Armadillo
15	**Arsinoitherium** (pharaoh name + "beast")	Great Pyramid and Sphinx of Giza, Egypt	Oligocene (27 mya)	Elephant, manatee
16	**Desmostylus**	Golden Gate Bridge, San Francisco, USA	Late Miocene (7.2 mya)	Elephant, manatee, hippo
17	〰 **Andrewsarchus** (explorer name + "leader")	Great Wall of China	Middle Eocene (41 mya)	Hippo, deer, pig
18	**Aepycamelus** ("high camel")	Hollywood Sign, Los Angeles, USA	Late Miocene (4.9 mya)	Camel
19	**Deinogalerix**	Colosseum, Rome, Italy	Late Miocene (7 mya)	Hedgehog
20	**Amphicyon** ("around dog") aka beardog	Chouara Tannery, Fes, Morocco	Late Pliocene (2.6 mya)	Bear, dog
21	**Ceratogaulus** aka horned gopher	Mount Rushmore, South Dakota, USA	Pliocene (4.9 mya)	Gopher
22	**Peltephilus** aka horned armadillo	Mi Teleférico (cablecar), La Paz, Bolivia	Middle Miocene (11.6 mya)	Armadillo
23	**Diprotodon** ("two forward teeth") aka giant wombat	Sydney Opera House, Australia	Late Pleistocene (44,000 ya)	Wombat, koala
24	**Hipparion** ("pony")	Burj Al Arab, Dubai, UAE	Middle Pleistocene (1 mya)	Horse
25	**Smilodon** aka sabre-toothed tiger	Times Square, New York City, USA	Late Pleistocene (10,000 ya)	Leopard

〰 = oldest extinction

T0018664

SPOTS

⏱ *Time to travel...*

1 *Deinotherium* · Parthenon, Athens, Greece · 2.6 million years ago

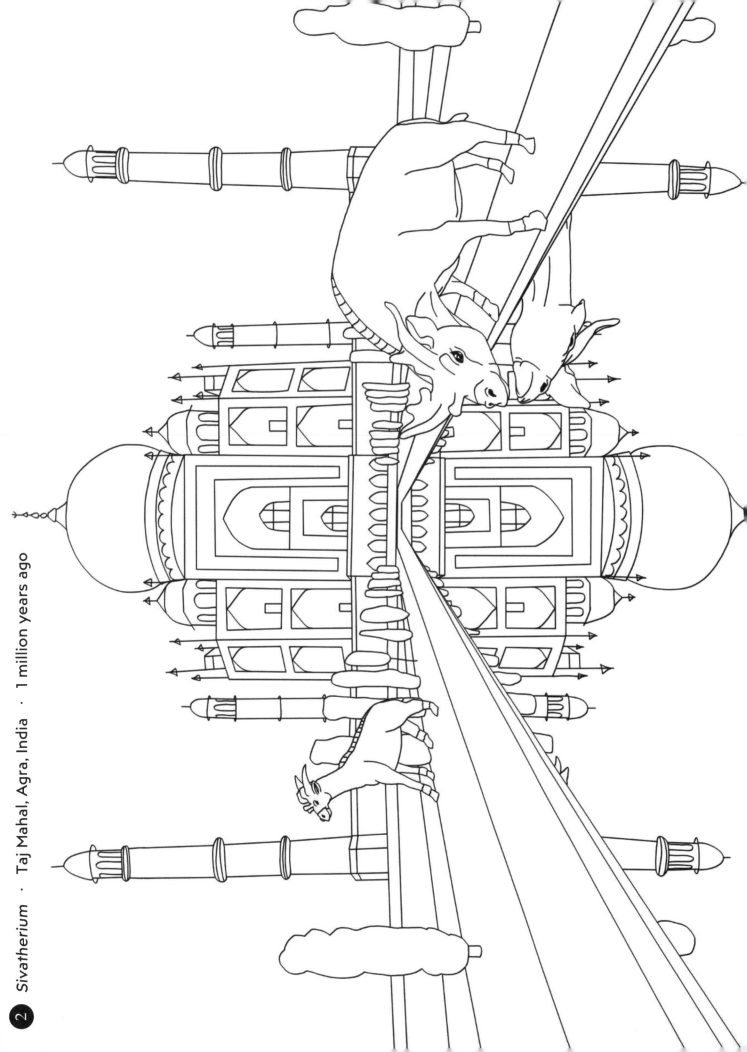

2 *Sivatherium* · Taj Mahal, Agra, India · 1 million years ago

Chalicotherium · East Side Gallery, Berlin, Germany · 3.6 million years ago

3

Macrauchenia · Machu Picchu, Peru · 15,000 years ago

4

Coelodonta · Amsterdam, Netherlands · 10,000 years ago

5

Gigantopithecus
Jardine House, Hong Kong · 300,000 years ago

Kretzoiarctos · Park Güell, Barcelona, Spain · 10 million years ago

Paraceratherium · Blue Mosque, Istanbul, Turkey · 23 million years ago

8

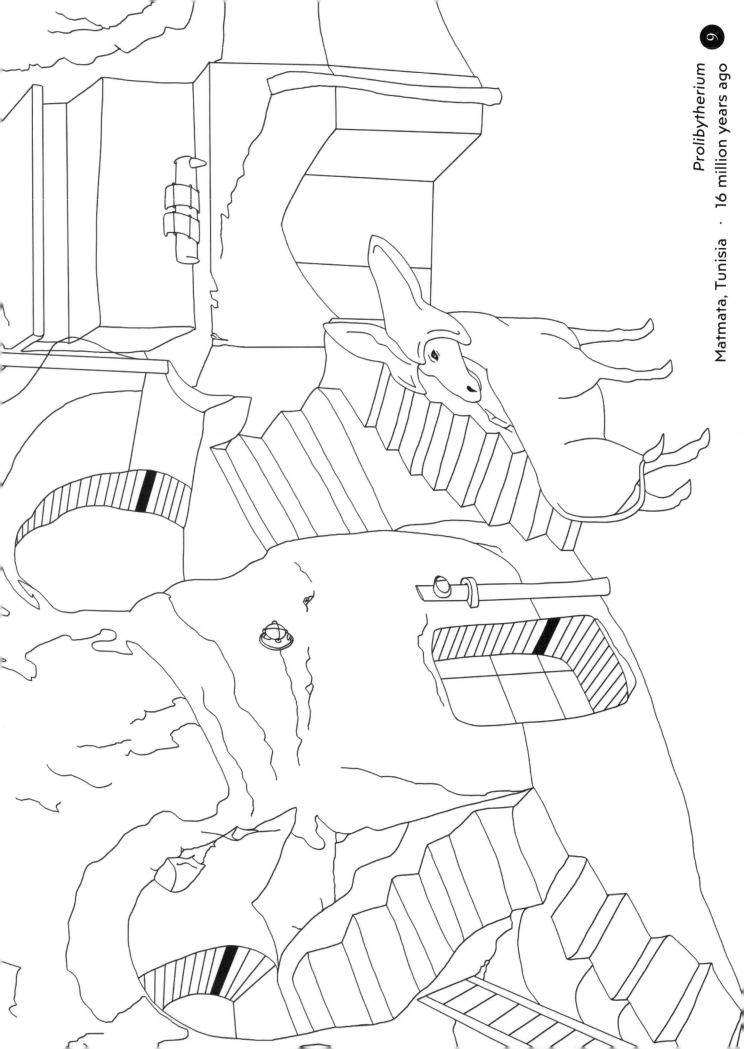

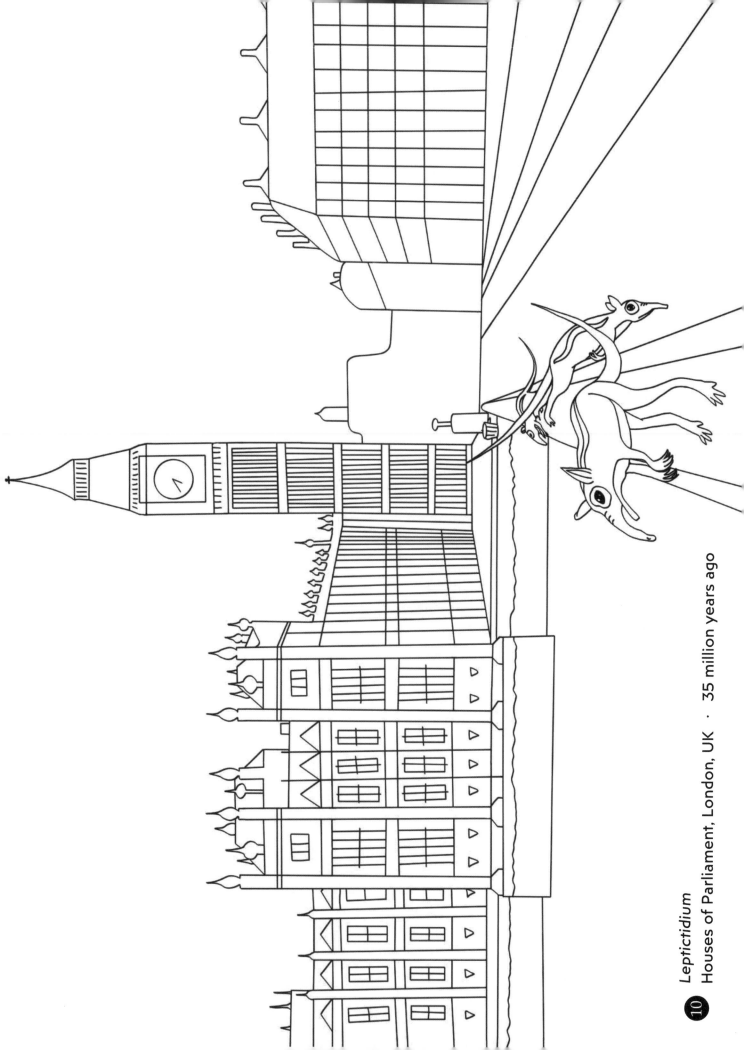

Leptictidium
Houses of Parliament, London, UK · 35 million years ago

10

Entelodon · Fushimi Inari Shrine, Kyoto, Japan · 28 million years ago

Eremotherium
Walt Disney World, Florida, USA
11,000 years ago

12

Eucladoceros · Moscow Metro, Russia · 2 million years ago

Glyptodon · Christ the Redeemer, Rio de Janeiro, Brazil · 11,000 years ago

Arsinoitherium · Great Pyramid and Sphinx of Giza, Egypt · 27 million years ago

15

Desmostylus · Golden Gate Bridge, San Francisco, USA · 7.2 million years ago

Aepycamelus · Hollywood Sign, Los Angeles, USA · 4.9 million years ago

19 *Deinogalerix* · Colosseum, Rome, Italy · 7 million years ago

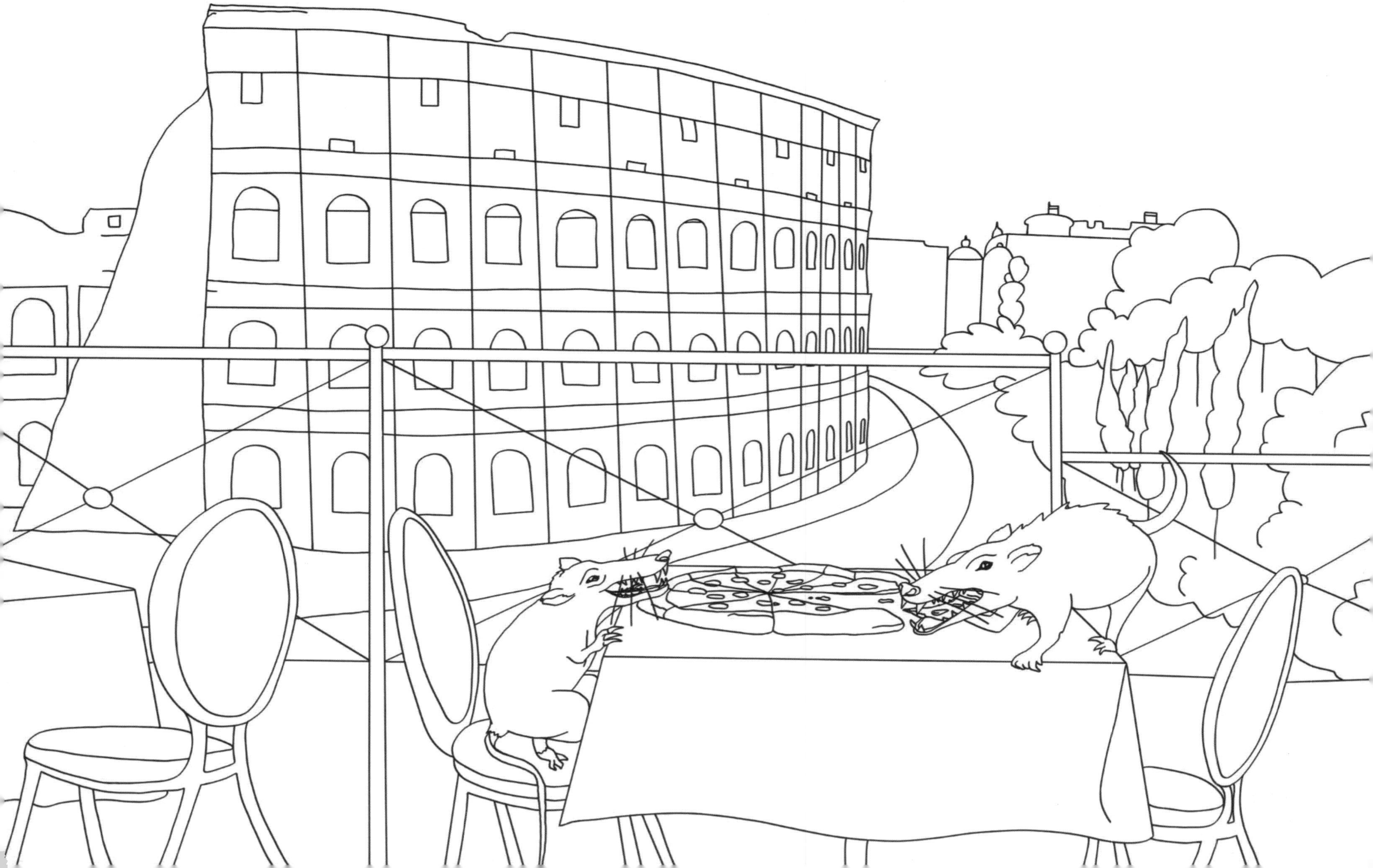

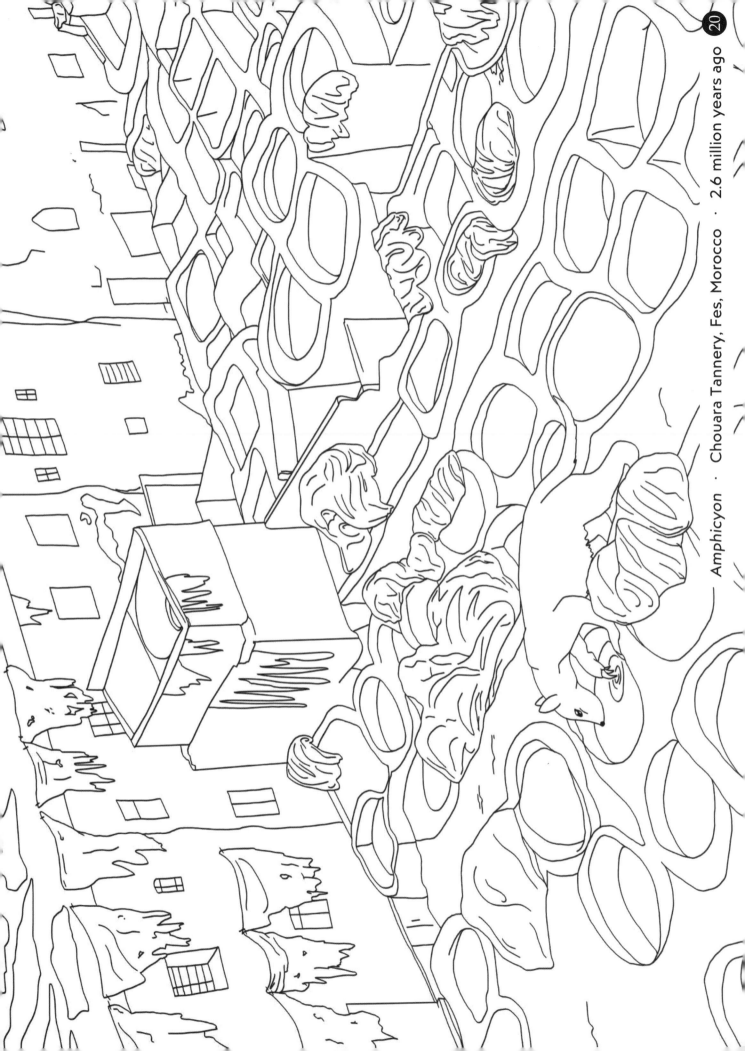

Amphicyon · Chouara Tannery, Fes, Morocco · 2.6 million years ago

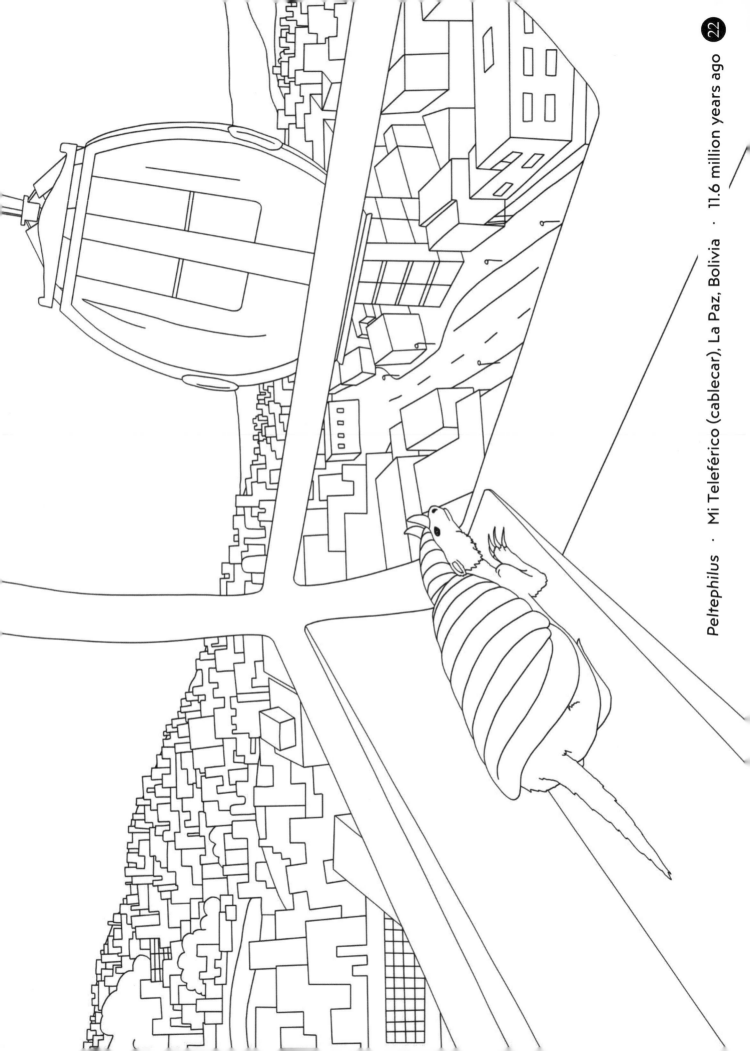

Peltephilus · Mi Teleférico (cablecar), La Paz, Bolivia · 11.6 million years ago

23 · Diprotodon · Sydney Opera House, Australia · 44,000 years ago

24 *Hipparion* · Burj Al Arab, Dubai, UAE · 1 million years ago

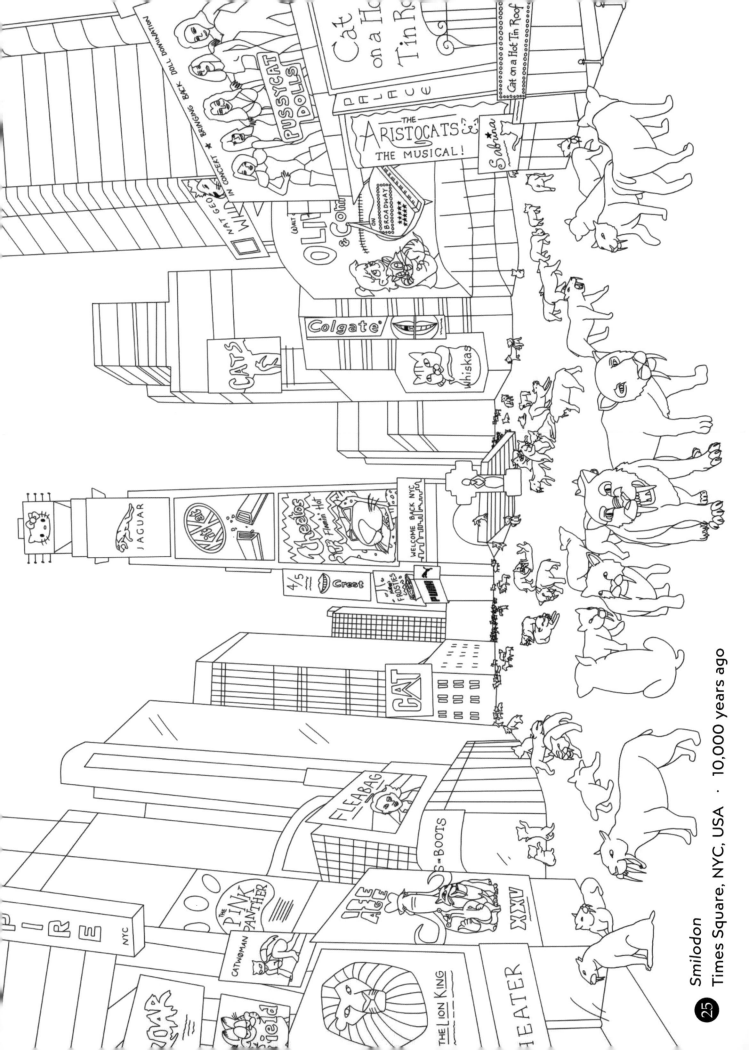

Smilodon
Times Square, NYC, USA · 10,000 years ago

25

— Thank You For Travelling PALAEO ERALINES ! —

Mammuthus · Astrapotherium · Xenokeryx · Josephoartigasia · Eobasileus
N. hemisphere · S. America · Spain · Uruguay · Mid-USA
4,000 ya · 11.6 mya · 20 mya · 1 mya · 40 mya